Informing the legislative debate since 1914 _____

National Security Letters: Proposal in the 113th Congress

Charles Doyle
Senior Specialist in American Public Law

November 22, 2013

Congressional Research Service

7-5700

www.crs.gov

R43322

Summary

National Security Letters (NSLs) are roughly comparable to administrative subpoenas. Various intelligence agencies use them to demand certain customer information from communications providers, financial institutions, and consumer credit reporting agencies under the Right to Financial Privacy Act, the Fair Credit Reporting Act, the National Security Act, and the Electronic Communications Privacy Act.

The bills in the 113ᵗʰ Congress that would amend the NSL statutes fall into four categories: (1) the grounds for issuing an NSL; (2) confidentiality requirements and judicial review; (3) reports and audits; and (4) sunset and repeal. S. 1551 (Wyden) and H.R. 3361 (Sensenbrenner)/ S. 1599 (Leahy) would define more precisely the circumstances under which an NSL might be issued.

Initially, the U.S. Court of Appeals for the Second Circuit and later the District Court for the Northern District of California concluded that the statutory secrecy and judicial review provisions relating to NSLs, read to their fullest, are inconsistent with the proscriptions of the First Amendment right to free speech and the principles of separation of powers. S. 1215 (Leahy) and H.R. 3361/S. 1599 would amend the provisions in question roughly along lines suggested by the Second Circuit.

In the past, Congress has counterbalanced expanded NSL authority with increased oversight mechanisms. For example, it directed the Department of Justice's Inspector General to conduct an audit of NSL authority from 2001 to 2006, and instructed the Attorney General to report to Congress annually on the extent of NSL use. Several proposals would supplement the existing mechanisms. S. 1215, S. 1551, and H.R. 3361/S. 1599 would call for greater detail in the Attorney General's annual reports. H.R. 3035 (Lofgren), S. 1551, and H.R. 3361/S. 1599 would authorize recipients to issue public reports on the NSLs they receive.

As an additional oversight tool, S. 1215 and H.R. 3361/S. 1599 would return all but two of the NSL statutes to the pre-USA PATRIOT Act form, effective June 1, 2015. The exceptions are the National Security Act NSL statute, which evokes few privacy concerns, and the sweeping, USA PATRIOT Act-born, Fair Credit Reporting Act NSL statute, which the bills would repeal.

This report reprints the text of the five NSL statutes as they now appear and as they appeared prior to amendment by the USA PATRIOT Act (to which form they would be returned under S. 1125 and H.R. 1805). Related reports include CRS Report R40138, *Amendments to the Foreign Intelligence Surveillance Act (FISA) Extended Until June 1, 2015*, by Edward C. Liu, and CRS Report RL33320, *National Security Letters in Foreign Intelligence Investigations: Legal Background*, by Charles Doyle.

Contents

Tables

Contacts

Introduction

National Security Letters (NSLs) are roughly comparable to administrative subpoenas. They need no prior judicial approval. Intelligence agencies issue them for intelligence gathering purposes to telephone companies, Internet service providers, consumer credit reporting agencies, banks, and other financial institutions, directing the recipients to turn over certain customer records and similar information. The 111th and 112th Congresses saw a number of proposals to amend NSL authority.[1] None were enacted. In the 112th Congress, they were closely associated with the scheduled expiration of various provisions of the Foreign Intelligence Surveillance Act (FISA).[2] In the 113th Congress, they have often been grouped with legislation that addresses the exercise of FISA authority.

Background

Prior to the USA PATRIOT Act, the NSL statutes were four. One, 18 U.S.C. 2709, obligated communications providers to supply certain customer information upon the written request of the Director of the Federal Bureau of Investigation (FBI) or a senior FBI headquarters official.[3] When customer identity, length of service, and toll records were sought, the letters had to certify (1) that the information was relevant to a foreign counterintelligence investigation and (2) that specific and articulable facts gave reason to believe the information pertained to a foreign power or its agents.[4] When only customer identity and length of service records (but not toll records) were sought, the letters had to certify (1) again that the information was relevant to a foreign counterintelligence investigation, but (2) that specific and articulable facts gave reason to believe that the customer information pertained to use of the provider's facilities to communicate with

---

[1] S.Rept. 111-92 (2009); S.Rept. 112-13 (2011); see generally, CRS Report R40887, *National Security Letters: Proposed Amendments in the 111th Congress*, by Charles Doyle, and CRS Report R41619, *National Security Letters: Proposals in the 112th Congress*, by Charles Doyle, from which this report borrows heavily.

[2] The so-called "lone wolf," "roving wiretap," and "section 215" amendments to FISA were scheduled to expire May 27, 2011. The temporary roving wiretap and section 215 provisions had originated in the USA PATRIOT Act, P.L. 107-56 (2001) and were first scheduled to expire on December 31, 2005. Congress extended their expiration date and that of the lone wolf provision on several occasions:

- from December 31, 2005, to February 3, 2006 (P.L. 109-160, 119 Stat. 2957(2005))
- from February 3, 2006, to March 10, 2006 (P.L. 109-170, 120 Stat. 3 (2006))
- from March 10, 2006, to December 31, 2009 (P.L. 109-177, 120 Stat. 194-95 (2006))
- from December 31, 2009, to February 28, 2010 (P.L. 111-118, 123 Stat. 3470 (2009))
- from February 28, 2010, to February 28, 2011 (P.L. 111-141, 124 Stat. 37 (2010))
- from February 28, 2011, to May 27, 2011 (P.L. 112-3, 125 Stat. 5 (2011)) and finally
- from May 27, 2011, to June 1, 2015 (P.L. 112-14, 125 Stat. 216 (2011)).

Although the Senate Judiciary Committee reported out legislation that would have addressed both the sunset of the three FISA provisions and NSL amendments, S.Rept. 112-13, Congress ultimately extended the expiring provisions in P.L. 112-14, without the NSL amendments. See generally, S.Rept. 112-13, at 2-12 (2011); CRS Report R40138, *Amendments to the Foreign Intelligence Surveillance Act (FISA) Extended Until June 1, 2015*, by Edward C. Liu.

[3] 18 U.S.C. 2709(a), (b) (2000 ed.).

[4] 18 U.S.C. 2709(b)(1) (2000 ed.).

foreign powers, their agents, or those engaged in international terrorism or criminal clandestine intelligence activities.[5]

In like manner a second statute, §1114(a)(5) of the Right to Financial Privacy Act, obligated financial institutions to provide the FBI with customers' financial records upon written certification of the FBI Director or his designee (1) that the records were sought for foreign counterintelligence purposes and (2) that specific and articulable facts gave reason to believe that the records were those of a foreign power or its agents.[6]

And so it was with a third, §626 of the Fair Credit Report Act, which obligated consumer credit reporting agencies to provide customer identification, and the names and addresses of financial institutions at which a designated consumer maintained accounts.[7] Here too, the obligation was triggered by written certification of the FBI Director or his designee (1) that the information was necessary for a foreign counterintelligence investigation, and (2) that specific and articulable facts gave reason to believe that the consumer was either a foreign power, a foreign official, or the agent of a foreign power and was engaged in international terrorism or criminal clandestine intelligence activities.[8]

The fourth, §802 of the National Security Act, was a bit different.[9] It reached a wider range of potential recipients at the demand of a large group of federal officials, but for a more limited purpose. It rested the obligation to provide consumer reports, together with financial information and records, upon consumer reporting agencies, financial agencies, and financial institutions, or holding companies.[10] The requirement was triggered by the certification of senior officials of law enforcement and intelligence agencies, but confined to information pertaining to federal employees with access to classified information and being sought for clearance purposes and inquiries into past or potential security leaks.[11]

USA PATRIOT Act

Section 505 of the USA PATRIOT Act altered the FBI's NSL authority under §2709 (communications information), the Right to Financial Privacy Act (financial information), and the Fair Credit Reporting Act (consumer credit information) in several ways:

- it expanded issuing authority to include the heads of FBI field offices (special agents in charge (SACs));

- it eliminated the requirement of specific and articulable facts demonstrating a nexus to a foreign power or its agents;

- it required instead that the information was sought for or relevant to various national security investigations; and

---

[5] 18 U.S.C. 2709(b)(2) (2000 ed.).

[6] 12 U.S.C. 3414(a)(5) (2000 ed.).

[7] 15 U.S.C. 1681u(a), (b) (2000 ed.).

[8] Id.

[9] 50 U.S.C. 436 (2000 ed.).

[10] Id.

[11] Id.

- It directed that no NSL related investigation of a "U.S. person" (American citizen or foreign resident alien) be predicated exclusively on First Amendment protected activities.[12]

The National Security Act NSL section remained unchanged, but §358(g) of the USA PATRIOT Act added a new Fair Credit Reporting Act NSL §627, 15 U.S.C. 1681v. The new section obligated consumer reporting agencies to provide consumer information and reports to a federal agency "authorized to conduct investigations of, or intelligence or counterintelligence activities or analysis related to, international terrorism."[13] Senior federal agency officials were empowered to issue the NSL with a certification that the information was "necessary for the agency's conduct or such investigation, activity, or analysis."[14]

2006 Amendments

Several of the USA PATRIOT Act's intelligence gathering provisions were temporary and originally set to expire after five years.[15] The NSL statutes were not among them, but Congress amended the NSL statutes in the USA PATRIOT Improvement and Reauthorization Act of 2005 and the USA PATRIOT Act Additional Reauthorizing Amendments Act of 2006 nonetheless.[16] The NSL amendments were driven both by sensitivity to an Administration desire for more explicit enforcement authority[17] and by judicial developments which had raised questions as to the statutes' constitutional vitality as then written.[18] The early statutes came with open-ended nondisclosure provisions which barred recipients from disclosing the fact or content of the NSL—to anyone, ever. Yet, they featured neither a penalty provision should the confidential requirement be breached or in most cases an enforcement mechanism should an NSL obligation

---

[12] Thus for example, section 626 of the Fair Credit Report Act, once stated in part that:

> The Director or the Director's designee may make such a certification only if [he or she] has determined in writing that—(1) such information is necessary for the conduct of an authorized foreign counterintelligence investigation; and (2) there are specific and articulable facts giving reason to believe that the consumer—(A) is a foreign power ... or a person who is not a United States person ... and is an official of a foreign power; or (b) is an agent of a foreign power and is engaging or has engaged in an act of international terrorism ... or clandestine intelligence activities that involve or may involve a violation of criminal statutes of the United States, 15 U.S.C. 1681u(a) (2000 ed.).

The USA PATRIOT Act redesignated section 626 as section 625 and the amended provision stated that:

> The Director or the Director's designee in a position not lower than Deputy Assistant Director at Bureau headquarters or Special Agent in Charge of a Bureau field office designated by the Director may make such a certification only if [he or she] has determined in writing that such information is sought for the conduct of an authorized investigation to protect against international terrorism or clandestine intelligence activities, provided that such an investigation of a United States person is not conducted solely upon the basis of activities protected by the first amendment to the Constitution of the United States, U.S.C. 1681u(a)(2000 ed. Supp. I).

[13] 15 U.S.C. 1681v(a)(2000 ed. Supp. I).

[14] *Id.*

[15] Sec. 224, P.L. 107-56, 115 Stat. 295 (2001).

[16] P.L. 109-177, 120 Stat. 192 (2006); P.L. 109-178, 120 Stat. 278 (2006), respectively.

[17] E.g., Anti-Terrorism Intelligence Tools Improvement Act of 2003: Hearing Before the Subcomm. on Crime, Terrorism, and Homeland Security, 108th Cong., 2d Sess. 7-8 (2004)(prepared statement of U.S. Ass't Att'y Gen. Daniel J. Bryant).

[18] *Doe v. Ashcroft*, 334 F.Supp.2d 471 (S.D.N.Y. 2004)(First and Fourth Amendment concerns); *Doe v. Gonzales*, 386 F.Supp.2d 66 (D. Conn. 2005)(First Amendment concerns).

---

be ignored (the original Fair Credit Report Act statute alone had an explicit judicial enforcement component).

The amendments:

- created a judicial enforcement mechanism and a judicial review procedure for both the requests and accompanying nondisclosure requirements;[19]
- established specific penalties for failure to comply with the nondisclosure requirements;[20]
- made it clear that the nondisclosure requirements did not preclude a recipient from consulting an attorney;[21]
- provided a process to ease the nondisclosure requirement;[22]
- expanded congressional oversight;[23] and
- called for Inspector General's audits of use of NSL authority.[24]

IG Reports

The First IG Report

The Department of Justice Inspector General reports, one released in March of 2007, the second in March of 2008, and the third in January of 2010, were less than totally favorable.[25] The first report noted that FBI use of NSLs had increased dramatically, expanding from 8,500 requests in 2000 to 47,000 in 2005, *IG Report I* at 120. During the three years under review, the percentage of NSLs used to investigate Americans ("U.S. persons") increased from 39% in 2003 to 53% in 2005.[26] A substantial majority of the requests involved records relating to telephone or e-mail communications.[27]

---

[19] 28 U.S.C. 3511.

[20] 28 U.S.C. 3511(c), 18 U.S.C. 1510(e).

[21] 12 U.S.C. 3414((a)(3)(A); 15 U.S.C. 1681v(c)(1), 1681u(d)(1); 18 U.S.C. 2709(c)(1); 50 U.S.C. 3162(B)(1)(prior to a recent reclassification this section appeared as 50 U.S.C. 436).

[22] 28 U.S.C. 3511(b).

[23] P.L. 109-177, §118.

[24] P.L. 109-177, §119.

[25] U.S. Department of Justice, Office of the Inspector General, *A Review of the Federal Bureau of Investigation's Use of National Security Letters* (*IG Report I*) (March 2007); *A Review of the FBI's Use of National Security Letters: Assessment of Corrective Actions and Examination of NSL Usage in 2006* (*IG Report II*) (March 2008); *A Review of the Federal Bureau of Investigation's Use of Exigent Letters and Other Informal Requests for Telephone Records* (*IG Report III*), all three available at http://www.usdoj.gov/oig/special/index htm.

[26] *Id.* A "U.S. person" is generally understood to mean "a citizen of the United States, an alien lawfully admitted for permanent residence (as defined in section 1101(a)(2) of title 8), an unincorporated association a substantial number of members of which are citizens of the United States or aliens lawfully admitted for permanent residence, or a corporation which is incorporated in the United States, but does not include a corporation or an association which is a foreign power, as defined in subsection(a)(1), (2), or (3) of this section," 50 U.S.C. 1801.

[27] *Id.*

The report and the subsequent report a year later provided a glimpse at how the individual NSL statutes were used and why they were considered valuable. In case of the 18 U.S.C. 2709, the Electronic Communications Privacy Act (ECPA) NSL statute, the reports explained that:

> Through national security letters, an FBI field office obtained telephone toll billing records and subscriber information about an investigative subject in a counterterrorism case. The information obtained identified the various telephone numbers with which the subject had frequent contact. Analysis of the telephone records enabled the FBI to identify a group of individuals residing in the same vicinity as the subject. The FBI initiated investigations on these individuals to determine if there was a terrorist cell operating in the city.[28]

> Headquarters and field personnel told us that the principal objective of the most frequently used type of NSL—ECPA NSLs seeking telephone toll billing records, electronic communication transactional records, or subscriber information (telephone and e-mail)—is to develop evidence to support applications for FISA orders.[29]

The Right to Financial Privacy Act (RFPA) NSL statute, 12 U.S.C. 3414(a)(5), also affords authorities access to a wide range of information (bank transaction records v. telephone transaction records) as demonstrated by the instances where it proved useful:

> The FBI conducted a multi-jurisdictional counterterrorism investigation of convenience store owners in the United States who allegedly sent funds to known Hawaladars (persons who use the Hawala money transfer system in lieu of or parallel to traditional banks) in the Middle East. The funds were transferred to suspected Al Qaeda affiliates. The possible violations committed by the subjects of these cases included money laundering, sale of untaxed cigarettes, check cashing fraud, illegal sale of pseudoephedrine (the precursor ingredient used to manufacture methamphetamine), unemployment insurance fraud, welfare fraud, immigration fraud, income tax violations, and sale of counterfeit merchandise.[30]

> The FBI issued national security letters for the convenience store owners' bank account records. The records showed that two persons received millions of dollars from the subjects and that another subject had forwarded large sums of money to one of these individuals. The bank analysis identified sources and recipients of the money transfers and assisted in the collection of information on targets of the investigation overseas.[31]

The Fair Credit Reporting Act NSL statutes, 15 U.S.C. 1681u (FCRAu) and 1681v (FCRAv) can be even more illuminating: "The supervisor of a counterterrorism squad told us that the FCRA NSLs enable the FBI to see 'how their investigative subjects conduct their day-to-day activities, how they get their money, and whether they are engaged in white collar crime that could be relevant to their investigations.'"[32]

Overall, the report notes that the FBI used the information gleaned from NSLs for a variety of purposes, "to determine if further investigation is warranted; to generate leads for other field

---

[28] *IG Report I* at 49.

[29] *IG Report II* at 65. The Foreign Intelligence Surveillance Act (FISA) authorizes the FBI to apply for court orders in national security cases authorizing electronic surveillance, physical searches, the installation and use of pen registers and trap and trace devices, and access to business records and other tangible property, 50 U.S.C. 1801-1862.

[30] Critics might suggest that these offenses are "possible" in the operation of any convenience store.

[31] *IG Report I* at 50.

[32] *Id.* at 51.

offices, Joint Terrorism Task Forces, or other federal agencies; and to corroborate information developed from other investigative techniques."[33] Moreover, information supplied in response to NSLs provides the grist of FBI analytical intelligence reports and various FBI databases.[34]

The report was somewhat critical, however, of the FBI's initial performance:

> [W]e found that the FBI used NSLs in violation of applicable NSL statutes, Attorney General Guidelines, and internal FBI policies. In addition, we found that the FBI circumvented the requirements of the ECPA NSL statute when it issued at least 739 "exigent letters" to obtain telephone toll billing records and subscriber information from three telephone companies without first issuing NSLs. Moreover, in a few other instances, the FBI sought or obtained telephone toll billing records in the absence of a national security investigation, when it sought and obtained consumer full credit reports in a counterintelligence investigation, and when it sought and obtained financial records and telephone toll billing records without first issuing NSLs.[35]

More specifically, the report found that:

- a "significant number of NSL-related possible violations were not being identified or reported" as required;

- the only FBI data collection system produced "inaccurate" results;

- the FBI issued over 700 exigent letters acquiring information in a manner that "circumvented the ECPA NSL statute and violated the Attorney General's Guidelines ... and internal FBI policy";

- the FBI's Counterterrorism Division initiated over 300 NSLs in a manner that precluded effective review prior to approval;

- 60% of the individual files examined showed violations of FBI internal control policies;

- the FBI did not retain signed copies of the NSLs it issued;

- the FBI had not provided clear guidance on the application of the Attorney General's least-intrusive-feasible-investigative-technique standard in the case of NSLs;

- the precise interpretation of toll billing information as it appears in the ECPA NSL statute is unclear;

- SAC supervision of the attorneys responsible for review of the legal adequacy of proposed NSLs made some of the attorneys reluctant to question the adequacy of the underlying investigation previously approved by the SAC;

- there was no indication that the FBI's misuse of NSL authority constituted criminal conduct;

- personnel both at FBI headquarters and in the field considered NSL use indispensable; and

---

[33] *Id.* at 65.

[34] *Id.*

[35] *Id.* at 124.

- information generated by NSLs was fed into a number of FBI systems.[36]

Exigent Letters

Prior to enactment of the Electronic Communications Privacy Act (ECPA), the Supreme Court held that customers had no Fourth Amendment protected privacy rights in the records the telephone company maintained relating to their telephone use.[37] Where a recognized expectation of privacy exists for Fourth Amendment purposes, the Amendment's usual demands such as those of probable cause, particularity, and a warrant may be eased in the face of exigent circumstances. For example, the Fourth Amendment requirement that officers must knock and announce their purpose before forcibly entering a building to execute a warrant can be eased in the presence of certain exigent circumstances such as the threat of the destruction of evidence or danger to the officers.[38] Satisfying Fourth Amendment requirements, however, does not necessarily satisfy statutory prohibitions.

The ECPA prohibits communications service providers from supplying information concerning customer records unless one of the statutory exceptions applies.[39] There are specific exceptions for disclosure upon receipt of a grand jury subpoena[40] or an NSL.[41] A service provider who knowingly or intentionally violates the prohibition is subject to civil liability,[42] but there are no criminal penalties for the breach.

The Inspector General found that contrary to assertions that "the FBI would obtain telephone records only after it served NSLs or grand jury subpoenas, the FBI obtained telephone bill records and subscriber information prior to serving NSLs or grand jury subpoenas" by using "exigent letters."[43] The FBI responded that it had barred the use of exigent letters, but emphasized that the term "exigent letter" does not include emergency disclosures under the exception now found in 18 U.S.C. 2702(c)(4). Thus, the FBI might request that a service provider invoke that exception to the record disclosure bar "if the provider reasonably believes that an emergency involving immediate danger of death or serious physical injury to any person justifies disclosure of the information."[44] Moreover, the Justice Department's Office of Legal Counsel subsequently advised the FBI in a classified memorandum that "under certain circumstances the ECPA does not prohibit electronic communications service providers from disclosing certain call detail records to the FBI on a voluntary basis without legal process or a qualifying emergency under Section 2702."[45]

---

[36] *IG Report I* at 121-24.

[37] *Smith v. Maryland*, 442 U.S. 735, 745 (1979)

[38] *Richards v. Wisconsin*, 520 U.S. 385, 391 (1997); *Wilson v. Arkansas*, 514 U.S. 927, 936 (1995).

[39] 18 U.S.C. 2702(c).

[40] 18 U.S.C. 2703(c)(2).

[41] 18 U.S.C. 2709(a).

[42] 18 U.S.C. 2707(a).

[43] *IG Report I* at 90.

[44] 18 U.S.C. 2702(c)(4).

[45] *Report by the Office of the Inspector General of the Department of Justice on the Federal Bureau of Investigation's Use of Exigent Letters and Other Informal Requests for Telephone Records: Hearing Before the Subcomm. on the Constitution, Civil Rights, and Civil Liberties of the House Comm. on the Judiciary*, 111th Cong. 2d sess. 22 (2010) (*2010 Hearings*) (statement of Department of Justice Inspector General Glenn Fine)(referring to a January 2010 OLC memorandum).

The Second IG Report

The second IG Report reviewed the FBI's use of national security letter authority during calendar year 2006 and the corrective measures taken following the issuance of the IG's first report. The second report concluded that:

- "the FBI's use of national security letters in 2006 continued the upward trend ... identified ... for the period covering 2003 through 2005";

- "the percentage of NSL requests generated from investigations of U.S. persons continued to increase significantly, from approximately 39% of all NSL requests issued in 2003 to approximately 57% of all NSL requests issued in 2006";

- the FBI and DOJ are committed to correcting the problems identified in *IG Report I* and "have made significant progress in addressing the need to improve compliance in the FBI's use of NSLs"; and

- "it [was] too early to definitively state whether the new systems and controls developed by the FBI and the Department will eliminate fully the problems with NSLs that we identified."[46]

The Third IG Report

The third IG Report examined the FBI's use of exigent letters and other informal means of acquiring communication service providers' customer records rather than relying on NSL authority during the period from 2003 to 2007.[47] The IG's Office discovered that "the FBI's use of exigent letters became so casual, routine, and unsupervised that employees of all three communications service providers sometimes generated exigent letters for FBI personnel to sign and return to them."[48]

Some of the informality was apparently the product of proximity. In order to facilitate cooperation, communications providers had assigned employees to FBI offices. In addition to a relaxed exigent letter process, the on-site feature gave rise to a practice of sneak peeks, that is, of providing the FBI with "a preview of the available information for a targeted phone number, without documentation of any justification for the request."[49] "In fact, at times the service providers' employees simply invited FBI personnel to view the telephone records on their computer screens. One senior FBI counterterrorism official described the culture of casual requests for telephone records by observing, 'It [was] like having the ATM in your living room.'"[50]

Not surprisingly, the IG's review

> found widespread use by the FBI of exigent letters and other informal requests for telephone records. These other requests were made ... without first providing legal process or even

---

[46] *IG Report II* at 8-9.

[47] *IG Report III* at 1.

[48] *2010 Hearings* at 14 (statement of Department of Justice Inspector General Glenn Fine).

[49] *Id.* at 15.

[50] *Id.*

exigent letters. The FBI also obtained telephone records through improper 'sneak peeks,' community of interest ███, and hot-number ███ Many of these practices violated FBI guidelines, Department policy, and the ECPA statute. In addition, we found that the FBI also made inaccurate statements to the FISA Court related to its use of exigent letters.[51]

Although critical of the FBI's initial response and recommending further steps to prevent reoccurrence, the IG's Report concluded that "the FBI took appropriate action to stop the use of exigent letters and to address the problems created by their use."[52]

Secrecy, Judicial Review, and the Judicial Reaction

At least for the time being, the current secrecy and judicial review provisions applicable to NSLs must be read in light of the Second Circuit's *John Doe, Inc. v. Mukasey* decision.[53] Under the NSL statutes, secrecy is not absolutely required. Instead, NSL recipients are bound to secrecy only upon the certification of the requesting agency that disclosure of the request or response may result in a danger to national security; may interfere with diplomatic relations or with a criminal, counterterrorism, or counterintelligence investigation; or may endanger the physical safety of an individual.[54] A recipient may disclose the request to those necessary to comply with the request and to an attorney the recipient consults for related legal advice or assistance.[55] In doing so, the recipient must advise them of the secrecy requirements.[56] Aside from its attorney the recipient must also identify, at the requesting agency's election, those to whom it has disclosed the request.[57]

Judicial Review of NSLs

Under the judicial review statute, 18 U.S.C. 3511, *a recipient may petition the court to modify or extinguish any NSL secrecy requirement* within a year of issuance.[58] Thereafter, it may petition to have the veil of secrecy lifted, although it may resubmit a rejected request only once a year.[59] Section 3511 provides that the court may modify or set aside the restriction if it finds "no reason to believe that disclosure may" endanger national security or personal safety or interfere with diplomatic relations or a criminal, counterterrorism, or counterintelligence investigation.[60] The

---

[51] *Id.* at 288 (redaction in the original).

[52] *IG Report III* at 289.

[53] 549 F.3d 861 (2d Cir. 2008). The observation here must be tempered because a district court in the Ninth Circuit, in an opinion and order stayed pending appeal, held that the Constitution precludes the exercise of the NSL statutes as currently configured, *In re National Security Letter*, 930 F.Supp.2d 1064, 1081 (N.D.Cal. 2013).

[54] *E.g.*, 18 U.S.C. 2709(c)(1). The other NSL statutes have comparable provisions. Nevertheless, "tens of thousands of NSLs are issued each year—and by the government's own estimate, 97% of them come with a nondisclosure order," *In re National Security Letter*, 930 F.Supp.2d at 1074.

[55] *Id.*

[56] *E.g.*, 12 U.S.C. 3414(a)(5)(D)(iii). The other NSL statutes have comparable provisions.

[57] *E.g.*, 15 U.S.C. 1681u(d)(4). The other NSL statutes have comparable provisions.

[58] 18 U.S.C. 3511(b)(2). As explained below, the Second Circuit opinion requires that the provisions in italics here and at the end of the paragraph be understood in the context of First Amendment demands.

[59] 18 U.S.C. 3511(b)(3).

[60] 18 U.S.C. 3511(b)(2), (3).

section, however, *binds the court to the assertion of a senior executive branch official that such an adverse consequence is possible.*[61]

In addition to authority to review and set aside NSL nondisclosure requirements, the federal courts also enjoy jurisdiction to review and enforce the underlying NSL requests. Section 3511 permits recipients to petition and authorizes the court to grant an order modifying or setting aside an NSL, if the court finds that compliance would be unreasonable, oppressive, or otherwise unlawful.[62] The "unreasonable or oppressive" standard is used for grand jury and other subpoenas issued under the Federal Rules of Criminal Procedure.[63] The Rules afford protection against undue burdens and protect privileged communications.[64] Compliance with a particular NSL might be unduly burdensome in some situations, but the circumstances under which NSLs are used suggest few federally recognized privileges. The Rules also impose a relevancy requirement, but in the context of a grand jury investigation a motion to quash will be denied unless it can be shown that "there is no reasonable possibility that the category of materials the Government seeks will produce information relevant" to the investigation.[65] The authority to modify or set aside an NSL that is "unlawful" affords the court an opportunity to determine whether the NSL in question complies with the statutory provisions under which it was issued. Section 3511 also vests the court with authority to enforce the NSL against a recalcitrant recipient. Failure to comply with the court's order thereafter is punishable as contempt of court.[66] A breach of a confidentiality requirement committed knowingly and with the intent to obstruct an investigation or related judicial proceedings is punishable by imprisonment for not more than five years and/or a fine of not more than $250,000 (not more than $500,000 for an organization).[67]

The Second Circuit concluded that the procedure can survive First Amendment scrutiny only if it involves the following:

- notice to NSL recipients that they may contest any secrecy order;

- expeditious government petition for judicial review of a secrecy order upon recipient request;

- government burden to establish the validity of its narrowly tailored secrecy order;

- no conclusive weight may be afforded governmental assertions; and

- recipients may apply or reapply annually for judicial review where the government's burden remains the same.[68]

On remand, the district upheld continuation of the nondisclosure order under the procedure suggested by the Second Circuit.[69]

---

[61] Id.

[62] 18 U.S.C. 3511(a).

[63] F.R.Crim.P. 17(c)(2).

[64] 2 WRIGHT, FEDERAL PRACTICE AND PROCEDURE §275 (Crim. 3d ed. 2000).

[65] *United States v. R. Enterprises, Inc.*, 498 U.S. 292, 301 (1991).

[66] 18 U.S.C. 3511(c).

[67] 18 U.S.C. 1510(e), 3571, 3559.

[68] *John Doe, Inc. v. Mukasey*, 549 F.3d 861, 883-84 (2d Cir. 2008).

[69] *Doe v. Holder*, 640 F.Supp. 2d 517 (S.D.N.Y. 2009); see also *Doe v. Holder*, 665 F.Supp. 2d 426 (S.D.N.Y. 2009)(finding continued compliance with the nondisclosure order justified); *Doe v. Holder*, 703 F.Supp.2d 313 (continued...)

The District Court for the Northern District of California agreed with the Second Circuit that the secrecy provisions as written violate the First Amendment and that the judicial review section as written violates both the First Amendment and separation of powers principles.[70] The court, however, did not agree that NSL authority might be exercised by reading into the statutes the constitutionally required limitations noted above.[71] Moreover, the court felt that constitutional defects in the confidentiality components of the NSL statutes invalidated the statutes as a whole.[72]

Table 1. Profile of the Current NSL Statutes

	18 U.S.C. 2709	12 U.S.C. 3414	15 U.S.C. 1681u	15 U.S.C. 1681v	50 U.S.C. 3162
Addressee	communications providers	financial institutions	consumer credit agencies	consumer credit agencies	financial institutions, consumer credit agencies, travel agencies
Certifying officials	senior FBI officials and SACs	senior FBI officials and SACs	senior FBI officials and SACs	supervisory official of an agency investigating, conducting intelligence activities relating to or analyzing international terrorism	senior officials no lower than Ass't Secretary or Ass't Director of agency with employees who have access to classified material
Information covered	identified customer's name, address, length of service, and billing information	identified customer financial records	identified consumer's name, address, former address, place and former place of employment	all information relating to an identified consumer	all financial information relating to consenting, identified employee
Standard/ Purpose	relevant to an investigation to protect against international terrorism or clandestine intelligence activities	sought for foreign counterintelligence purposes to protect against international terrorism or clandestine intelligence activities	sought for an investigation to protect against international terrorism or clandestine intelligence activities	necessary for the agency's investigation, activities, or analysis relating to international terrorism	necessary to conduct a law enforcement investigation, counterintelligence inquiry or security determination
Dissemination	only per Att'y Gen. guidelines	only per Att'y Gen. guidelines	within FBI, to secure approval for intelligence investigation, to	no statutory provision	only to agency of employee under investigation, DOJ for law

(...continued)

(S.D.N.Y. 2010)(permitting the disclosure of some related information).

[70] *In re National Security Letter*, 930 F.Supp.2d 1064, 1081 (N.D.Cal. 2013).

[71] *Id.* at 1080("The statutory provisions at issue – as written, adopted and amended by Congress in the face of a constitutional challenge – are not susceptible to narrowing conforming constructions to save their constitutionality ... [I]n amending and reenacting the statute as it did, Congress was concerned with giving the government the broadest powers possible to issue NSL nondisclosure orders and preclude searching judicial review of the same ... [T]he sorts of multiple inferences required to save the provisions at issue are not only contrary to evidence of Congressional intent, but also contrary to the statutory language and structure of the statutory provisions actually enacted by Congress").

[72] *Id.* at 1081("The Court also finds that the unconstitutional nondisclosure provisions are not severable").

	18 U.S.C. 2709	12 U.S.C. 3414	15 U.S.C. 1681u	15 U.S.C. 1681v	50 U.S.C. 3162
			military investigators when information relates to military member		enforcement or intelligence purposes, or federal agency when clearly relevant to mission
Immunity/fees	no provisions	no provisions	fees; immunity for good faith compliance with an NSL	immunity for good faith compliance with an NSL	reimbursement; immunity for good faith compliance with an NSL

Source: Congressional Research Service, based on statutes cited in the chart.

Proposed Amendments

Bills in this Congress that would amend the NSL statutes and related provisions fall into several categories: (1) the grounds for issuing an NSL; (2) confidentiality requirements, enforcement, and judicial review; (3) reports and audits; and (4) sunset and repeal. Some are focused on a single category; others are more comprehensive.

Grounds for Issuance

Prior to the USA PATRIOT Act, the communications, financial institution, and consumer credit NSL statutes each required certification by a senior FBI official that "specific and articulable" facts exist to support the belief that the relevant information sought related to a foreign power or the agent of a foreign power.[73] For instance, the communications provider NSL statute declared:

> The Director of the Federal Bureau of Investigation ... may - (1) request the name, address, length of service, and local and long distance toll billing records of a person or entity if the Director ... certifies in writing to the ... provider to which the request is made that - (A) the ... records sought are relevant to an authorized foreign counterintelligence investigation; and (B) there are *specific and articulable facts* giving reason to believe that the person or entity to whom the information sought pertains is a foreign power or an agent of a foreign power....[74]

The USA PATRIOT Act eliminated those requirements,[75] so that the amended communications NSL for example now states:

> The Director of the Federal Bureau of Investigation ... may - (1) request the name, address, length of service, and local and long distance toll billing records of a person or entity if the Director ... certifies in writing to the ... provider to which the request is made that the ...

---

[73] 12 U.S.C. 3414(a)(5)(2000 ed.); 15 U.S.C. 1681u(a)(2000 ed.); 18 U.S.C. 2709(b)(2000 ed.). USA PATRIOT Act added the second Fair Credit Reporting Act NSL, 15 U.S.C. 1681v, and the features of the National Security Act provisions, 50 U.S.C. 3162, are clearly distinct.

[74] 18 U.S.C. 2709(b)(1)(2000 ed.).

[75] P.L. 107-56, §505(a), (b), (c), 115 Stat. 365-66 (2001); 12 U.S.C. 3414(a)(5); 15 U.S.C. 1681u(a); 18 U.S.C. 2709(b).

records sought are relevant to an authorized investigation to protect against international terrorism or clandestine intelligence activities, provided that such an investigation of a United States person is not conducted solely on the basis of activities protected by the first amendment to the Constitution of the United States.[76]

A witness at an earlier congressional hearing indicated that the "specific and articulable" facts standard grew out of the standards employed in counterintelligence investigations and did not always translate well in a counterterrorism context:

> My point is that the "specific and articulable facts" standard was particularly suited to the counterintelligence operations of the era in which it was created. A FBI counterintelligence investigation involved examining a linear connection between a foreign intelligence officer (about whom much was known) and his contacts (potential spies). The information known about the intelligence officer was specific in nature, and could be readily used to meet the NSL legal standards.... Unlike the traditional linear counterintelligence case, in which the foreign agent tried to recruit the domestic spy using infrequent and highly secure forms of communication, many counterterrorism cases involved complex networks generating a much larger volume of communication and financial transactions. In counter-terrorism cases, the starting point was often not a clearly identifiable agent of a foreign power (as in counterintelligence); indeed, the relevant "foreign power" was itself an imperfectly understood terrorist organization that might defy precise definition. As a consequence, counter-terrorism investigators often had a far more difficult time meeting the "specific and articulable facts" standard.[77]

On the other hand, a later hearing witness argued that relaxation of the specific-and-articulable-facts standard eliminates an individualized suspicion requirement with the result that information is gathered about individuals who have a remote connection to a suspected foreign agent, at best.[78]

S. 1551 (Wyden) would reestablish the specific-and-articulable-facts standard in the three basic NSL statutes,[79] and would describe three categories of individuals whose records an NSL may reach: (A) foreign powers or their agents; (B) the activities of a suspected foreign agent who is the target of the investigation; or (C) "an individual in contact with, or known to, a suspected foreign agent."[80]

---

[76] 18 U.S.C. 2709(b)(1).

[77] *National Security Letters: The Need for Greater Accountability and Oversight: Hearing Before the Senate Comm. on the Judiciary*, 110th Cong., 2d sess. (2008)(testimony of Michael J. Woods, former Chief of the FBI's National Security Law Unit), available at http://judiciary.senate.gov/pdf/08-04-23WoodsTestimony.pdf.

[78] "[T]he executive branch is now using NSLs not only to investigate people who are known or suspected to present threats but also—and indeed principally—to collect information about innocent people. News reports indicate that the FBI has used NSLs to obtain data not only on individuals it saw as targets but also details on their 'community of interest'—the network of people that the target was in contact with," *Strengthening Privacy Rights and National Security: Oversight of FISA Surveillance Programs Accountability and Oversight: Hearing Before the Senate Comm. on the Judiciary*, 113th Cong., 1st sess. (2013)(testimony of Jameel Jaffer, Deputy Legal Director of the American Civil Liberties Union Foundation), available on October 23, 2009, at http://judiciary.senate.gov/pdf/7-31-13JafferTestimony.pdf.

[79] S. 1551 would repeal the second Fair Credit Report Act statute, the USA PATRIOT Act- born, 15 U.S.C. 1681v, S. 1551, §501(c)(2).

[80] E.g., S. 1551, §501(a)(1), proposed 18 U.S.C. 2709(b)("The Director of the Federal Bureau of Investigation ... or a Special Agent in Charge ... may (1) request the name, address, length of service, and local and long distance toll billing records of a person or entity if the Director (or the Director's designee) certifies in writing to the wire or electronic communications service provider to which the request is made that ... (B) there are specific and articulable facts (continued...)

Taking a somewhat similar approach, H.R. 3361 (Sensenbrenner)/S. 1599 (Leahy) would amend the three NSL statutes to include specific references to the three categories of individuals cited in S. 1551 whose records may be captured.[81] Like S. 1551, they would repeal the second, more sweeping, Fair Credit Report Act NSL statute, 16 U.S.C. 1681v.[82]

Instead of reestablishing the specific-and-articulable-facts standard, however, they would insist that the information sought—which now need only be "relevant to an authorized investigation to protect against international terrorism or clandestine intelligence activities"—be both relevant and material.[83] Information is relevant when it relates to a matter under investigation, when it has probative value.[84] It is material when it of sufficient significance to have the natural tendency to influence a decision.[85]

The bills would all preserve the post-USA PATRIOT Act prohibition on use of the authority in an investigation based solely on the basis of First Amendment-protected activities.[86]

Confidentiality and Judicial Review

Each of the NSL statutes has a nondisclosure provision.[87] They state that the issuing agency may prohibit recipients from ever disclosing the request to anyone other than their attorney and those necessary to comply with the request.[88] In order to activate the authority, agency officials must certify that disclosure may endanger national security or individual safety, or may interfere with diplomatic relations or with a criminal, counterintelligence, or counterterrorism investigation.[89]

The statutes declare that a federal district court may modify or set aside an NSL secrecy requirement on the petition of a recipient, if it concludes that there is no reason to believe that

---

(...continued)

showing that there are reasonable grounds to believe that the name, address, length of service, and toll billing records sought – (i) pertain to a foreign power or agent of a foreign power; (ii) are relevant to the activities of a suspected agent of a foreign power who is the subject of such authorized investigation; or (iii) pertain to an individual in contact with, or known to, a suspected agent"); §501(b), proposed 12 U.S.C. 3414(b)(1); §501(c)(1), proposed 1681u(b)(1).

[81] H.R. 3361/S. 1599, §§501(a)(2), 501(b), 501(c)(1); proposed 18 U.S.C. 2709(b)(2), proposed 12 U.S.C. 3414(b)(1)(B)(ii), proposed 15 U.S.C. 1681u(b)(1)(B)(ii).

[82] H.R. 3361/S. 1599, §501(c)(2).

[83] H.R. 3361/S. 1599, §§501(a)(1), 501(b), 501(c)(1); proposed 18 U.S.C. 2709(b)(1), proposed 12 U.S.C. 3414(b)(1)(B)(i), proposed 15 U.S.C. 1681u(b)(1)(B)(i).

[84] BLACK'S LAW DICTIONARY 1404 (9th ed. 2009)("relevance ... relation or pertinence to the issue at hand")("relevant ... having appreciable probative value.... "); note that in the context of a grand jury investigation, where "a subpoena is challenged on relevancy grounds, the motion to quash must be denied unless the district court determines that there is no reasonable possibility that the category of materials the Government seeks will produce information relevant to the general subject of the grand jury's investigation, " *United States v. R Enterprises, Inc.*, 498 U.S. 292, 301 (1991)); *In re Grand Jury Proceedings*, 616 F.3d 1186, 1202 (10th Cir.2010).

[85] BLACK'S LAW DICTIONARY 1066 (9th ed. 2009)("material ... of such a nature that knowledge of the item would affect a person's decision making process"); *United States v. Natale*, 719 F.3d 719, 735 (7th Cir. 2013); *United States v. Coplan*, 703 F.3d 46, (2d Cir. 2012).

[86] S. 1551, §501(a)(1), (b), (c)(1); H.R. 3361/S. 1599, §501(a)(1), (b), (c)(1); in each bill, proposed 18 U.S.C. 2709(b)(1), (2); proposed 12 U.S.C. 3414(b)(1); proposed 16 U.S.C. 1681u(b).

[87] 12 U.S.C. 3414(a)(5)(D); 18 U.S.C. 2709(c); 15 U.S.C. 1681u(d); 15 U.S.C. 1681v(c); 50 U.S.C. 3162(b).

[88] *Id.*

[89] *Id.*

---

disclosure might result in any such danger or interference.[90] If the petition for review is filed more than a year after issuance of the NSL, the agency must either terminate the gag order or recertify the need for its continuation.[91] They make no explicit provision for disclosure to the party to whom the information pertains.

The Second Circuit in *John Doe, Inc. v. Mukasey* held that these provisions only survive First Amendment scrutiny if the agency petitions for judicial review and convinces the court that the agency's proposed order is narrowly crafted to meet to the statutorily identified adverse consequences of disclosure.[92] The district court opinion in the Ninth Circuit, *In re National Security Letter*, now stayed pending appeal, concluded these confidentiality provisions are constitutionally invalid on their face and cannot be saved by tailored application within constitutional bounds.[93] Moreover, the district court opined that the provisions are not severable and consequently take down with them the NSL statutes of which they are a part.[94]

H.R. 3361 (Sensenbrener)/S. 1599 (Leahy) would modify the statutory provisions governing the issuance and judicial review of NSL nondisclosure orders. They would continue in place the personal safety and interference with diplomatic immunity grounds, but they would replace the references to risk of interference with a criminal, counterterrorism, or counterintelligence investigation with more specific grounds: the risk of flight, destruction of evidence, witness intimidation, or alerting the target of an investigation.[95] They would also narrow the danger-to-national-security justification to instances involving a risk of "substantial" danger to national security.[96]

The newly added specifics—destruction of evidence, suspect flight, and witness intimidation— are the kind of factors considered exigent circumstances in other contexts. As noted earlier, they permit entry to execute a warrant without first announcing the officers' purposes and authority, for instance.[97]

H.R. 3361/S. 1599 would amend the statutory provisions governing judicial review of NSLs and their nondisclosure orders.[98] They would codify a procedure comparable in many respects to that which the Second Circuit identified as constitutionally acceptable. The agency issuing the NSL would have made the initial determination of whether to include a nondisclosure provision in the NSL and that determination would be subject to judicial review.[99] They would include the

---

[90] 18 U.S.C. 3511(b)(1), (2).

[91] 18 U.S.C. 3511(b)(1), (3).

[92] 549 F.3d 861, 883 (2d Cir. 2008).

[93] 930 F.Supp.2d 1064, 1080 (N.D. Cal. 2013).

[94] *Id.* at 1081.

[95] H.R. 3361/S. 1599, §502(a), (b), (c), (d); proposed 18 U.S.C. 2709(c)(1); proposed 12 U.S.C. 3414(c)(1), proposed 15 U.S.C. 1681u(c)(1); proposed 50 U.S.C. 3162(b)(1).

[96] *Id.*

[97] *Richards v. Wisconsin*, 520 U.S. 385, 391 (1997); *Wilson v. Arkansas*, 514 U.S. 927, 936 (1995). See also, 18 U.S.C. 2705(a)(2)(factors justifying delayed notification of a court order directing a remote computing service provider to supply a governmental entity with provider copies of the content of customer e-mails); 3103a (justifications for "sneak and peek" warrants).

[98] H.R. 3361/S. 1599, §502(e); proposed 18 U.S.C. 3511(b).

[99] H.R. 3361/S. 1599, §502(a), (b), (c), (d); proposed 18 U.S.C. 2709(c)(1); proposed 15 U.S.C. 1681u(d)(1); proposed 12 U.S.C. 3414(c); proposed 50 U.S.C. 3162(b)(1).

expanded list of concerns a requesting official might rely upon in order to impose a nondisclosure order: reason to believe disclosure may substantially endanger national security or individual safety; interfere with diplomatic relations; result in flight, destruction of evidence, or witness intimidation; or alert a target of the investigation.[100]

The agency would have to notify the recipient of the right to judicial review and petition for review within 30 days of a recipient's request for judicial review.[101] The agency's application for judicial approval or review would have to include a statement of facts giving reason to believe that disclosure might result in one of the statutory list of adverse consequences—risk of substantially endangering national security or individual safety, destruction of evidence, etc.[102] Should the court feel the agency had met its burden, it would be required to issue a nondisclosure order.[103]

S. 1215 (Leahy) proposes many of the same alterations in the procedures governing the issuance and judicial review of nondisclosure orders. It would leave unchanged, however, the risks of adverse consequences upon which an official might base the decision to include a confidentiality requirement and upon which a court might approve one: danger to national security; interference with a criminal, counterterrorism, or counterintelligence investigation; interference with diplomatic relations; or individual safety.[104] Otherwise, the bill would require notice to recipient of the right to appeal a nondisclosure order[105] and impose the obligation to proceed within 30 days upon the government.[106] Unlike H.R. 3361/S. 1599, however, under S. 1215 the court would have to give "substantial weight" to the government's certification of the risk of adverse consequences of a failure to uphold the secrecy requirement.[107]

Reports and Audits

Two sections of the USA PATRIOT Improvement and Reauthorization Act called for NSL-related reports and audits. Some of the NSL statutes provide for periodic reports to various congressional committees.[108] Section 118(a) of the USA PATRIOT Improvement and Reauthorization Act added the House and Senate Judiciary Committees to the list of required recipients of such reports.[109] Section 118(c) directed the Attorney General to prepare, in unclassified form, an annual report to Congress on the number of NSLs issued in the previous year.[110] Section 119 directed the Inspector General of the Department of Justice to audit and report on the use of NSL authority for

---

[100] H.R. 3361/S1599, §502(a), (b), (c), (d); proposed 18 U.S.C. 2709(c)(1)(B); proposed 15 U.S.C. 1681u(d)(1)(B); proposed 12 U.S.C. 3414(c)(1)(B); proposed 50 U.S.C. 3162(b)(1)(B).

[101] H.R. 3361/S. 1599 §502(e); proposed 18 U.S.C. 3511(b).

[102] H.R. 3361/S. 1599, §502(e); proposed 18 U.S.C. 3511(b)(2).

[103] H.R. 3361/S. 1599, §502(e); proposed 18 U.S.C. 3511(b)(3).

[104] S. 1215, §5(a), (b), (c), (d), (e); proposed 18 U.S.C. 2709(c)(1); proposed 15 U.S.C. 1681u(d)(1); proposed 15 U.S.C. 1681v(c)(1); proposed 12 U.S.C. 3414(a)(5)(D)(i); proposed 50 U.S.C. 3162(b)(1).

[105] S. 1215, §5(a), (b), (c), (d), (e); proposed 18 U.S.C. 2709(c)(3); proposed 15 U.S.C. 1681u(d)(3); proposed 15 U.S.C. 1681v(c)(3); proposed 12 U.S.C. 3414(a)(5)(D)(iii); proposed 50 U.S.C. 3162(b)(3).

[106] S. 1215, §6(b); proposed 18 U.S.C. 3511(b)(1).

[107] S. 1215, §6(b); proposed 18 U.S.C. 3511(b)(3).

[108] 18 U.S.C. 2709(e); 15 U.S.C. 1681u(h); 15 U.S.C. 1681v(f).

[109] P.L. 109-177, §118(a), 120 Stat. 217 (2006), 18 U.S.C. 3511 note.

[110] P.L. 109-177, §118(c), 120 Stat. 218 (2006), 18 U.S.C. 3511 note.

---

calendar years 2002 through 2006.[111] A number of bills in the 113th Congress would expand one or both of the report and the audit requirements.

S. 1215 (Leahy), H.R. 3361 (Sensenbrenner)/S. 1599 (Leahy) each contemplate more detailed reports in both classified and unclassified forms.[112] The bills would require the Attorney General to submit each report to the House and Senate judiciary, intelligence, and banking committees twice a year on the number of NSL requests submitted during the reporting period that relate to each of several categories: U.S. persons; non-U.S. persons; subjects of an investigation; those who were linked to the subject of an investigation; and those not themselves the subject of an investigation.[113] The bills would eliminate the current exclusion of requests for communications subscriber information.[114]

S. 1551 (Wyden) would require a break down of reported totals according to U.S persons; non-U.S. persons; those who are the subject to the national security investigation; and those who are not the subject of such investigations.[115]

Several Members have suggested public reporting by the recipients of NSLs and Foreign Intelligence Surveillance Act (FISA) orders. Thus, H.R. 3035 (Lofgren), S. 1551 (Wyden), and H.R. 3361 (Sensenbrenner)/S. 1599 (Leahy) each allow electronic service providers to issue periodic reports on the number of NSL requests they receive, organized according to the NSL statute under which the requests were received or by categories of the authorizing statutes.[116] They would also immunize providers from civil and criminal liability for any good faith exercise of the authority the bills would provide.[117]

Section 119 called an NSL audit by the Department of Justice Inspector General for the time period covering 2002 through 2006.[118] S. 1215 (Leahy) and H.R. 3361 (Sensenbrenner)/ S. 1599 (Leahy) would call for a similar audit covering 2010 through 2013.[119] The bills call for audits by the intelligence community Inspectors General as well. In the case of S. 1215, these intelligence assessments would be conducted by the Inspectors General of the various agencies of the intelligence community.[120] In the case of H.R. 3361/S. 1599, the Inspector General of the Intelligence Community would perform the assessment.[121] In either case, the audit would cover the period from 2010 to 2013 and would include (a) an assessment of the importance of NSL

---

[111] P.L. 109-177, §119, 120 Stat. 219 (2006).

[112] S. 1215, §8, proposed §118(c)(USA PATRIOT Improvement and Reauthorization Act), 18 U.S.C. 3511 note; H.R. 3361/S. 1599, §603, proposed §118(c)(USA PATRIOT Improvement and Reauthorization Act), 18 U.S.C. 3511 note.

[113] S. 1215, §8(a), proposed §118(c)(1), (2), (3)(USA PATRIOT Improvement and Reauthorization Act), 18 U.S.C. 3511 note; H.R. 3361/S. 1599, §603, proposed §118(c)(1), (2), (3)(USA PATRIOT Improvement and Reauthorization Act), 18 U.S.C. 3511 note.

[114] S. 1215, §8(a), proposed §118(c)(1)(USA PATRIOT Improvement and Reauthorization Act), 18 U.S.C. 3511 note; H.R. 3361/S. 1599, §603(a), proposed §118(c)(1)(USA PATRIOT Improvement and Reauthorization Act), 18 U.S.C. 3511 note.

[115] S. 1551, §502(3) proposed §118(c)(2)(USA PATRIOT Improvement and Reauthorization Act), 18 U.S.C. 3511 note.

[116] H.R. 3035, §2; S. 1551, §601; H.R. 3361/S. 1599, §601.

[117] H.R. 3035, §2(d); S. 1551, §601(d); H.R. 3361/S. 1599, §601(d).

[118] P.L. 109-177, §119, 120 Stat. 219 (2006).

[119] S. 1215, §10(b); H.R. 3361/S. 1599, §504; proposed §119(USA PATRIOT Improvement and Reauthorization Act).

[120] S. 1215, §10(b), proposed §119(d)(USA PATRIOT Improvement and Reauthorization Act).

[121] H.R. 3361/S. 1599, §504(d), proposed §119(d)(USA PATRIOT Improvement and Reauthorization Act).

information; (b) inquiry into the manner of NSL information collection, retention, analysis, and dissemination; (c) point out any noteworthy acts (including in the case of H.R. 3361/S. 1599, and any improper or illegal practices); and (d) look into the use of NSLs (or in the case of S. 1215, examine the minimization procedures used).[122]

Sunset and Repeal

Section 627 of the Fair Credit Reporting Act, the NSL statute created in the USA PATRIOT Act,[123] is arguably the most sweeping of the NSL statutes. It offers the most extensive array of information (all information pertaining to a consumer held by a consumer credit reporting agency) to the widest range of requesters (any federal agency "authorized to conduct investigations of, or intelligence or counterintelligence activities or analysis relating to, international terrorism").[124]

Several bills would repeal it.[125] Its repeal might be seen to facilitate oversight, since it would centralize authority to issue NSLs in the FBI (other than in the case of employee security investigations under the National Security Act). Moreover, the Justice Department IG reported that both the FBI and consumer reporting agencies had experienced difficulty distinguishing between authority under 1681u and 1681v.[126]

Congress has not previously made either the NSL statutes or their USA PATRIOT Act amendments temporary. S. 1215 (Leahy) and H.R. 3361 (Sensenbrenner)/S. 1599 (Leahy) would change that. Effective June 1, 2015, the bills would return NSL statutes to their pre-USA PATRIOT Act form.[127] They would establish a transition provision under which the law prior to May 31, 2015, would continue to apply with respect to investigations or offenses begun prior to June 1, 2015.[128]

---

[122] S. 1215, §10(b); H.R. 3361/S. 1599, §504, proposed §119(d)(USA PATRIOT Improvement and Reauthorization Act).

[123] P.L. 107-56, §358(g), 115 Stat. 327 (2001), 15 U.S.C. 1681v.

[124] 15 U.S.C. 1681v(a). Such agencies would presumably include at a minimum those agencies who are members of the "intelligence community," see e.g., 50 U.S.C. 401a(4)("The term 'intelligence community' includes the following: (A) The Office of the Director of National Intelligence. (B) The Central Intelligence Agency. (C) The National Security Agency. (D) The Defense Intelligence Agency. (E) The National Geospatial-Intelligence Agency. (F) The National Reconnaissance Office. (G) Other offices within the Department of Defense for the collection of specialized national intelligence through reconnaissance programs. (H) The intelligence elements of the Army, the Navy, the Air Force, the Marine Corps, the Federal Bureau of Investigation, and the Department of Energy. (I) The Bureau of Intelligence and Research of the Department of State. (J) The Office of Intelligence and Analysis of the Department of the Treasury. (K) The elements of the Department of Homeland Security concerned with the analysis of intelligence information, including the Office of Intelligence of the Coast Guard. (L) Such other elements of any other department or agency as may be designated by the President, or designated jointly by the Director of National Intelligence and the head of the department or agency concerned, as an element of the intelligence community"). Admittedly, section 1681v only identifies those who may invoke NSL authority, not necessarily those who have or will exercise that authority.

[125] H.R. 3361 (Sensenbrenner)/S. 1599 (Leahy), §501(c)(2); S. 1551 (Wyden), §501(c)(2); see also, H.R. 2818 (Holt), §2 ("The USA PATRIOT Act (P.L. 107-56) is repealed.... ").

[126] *IG Report I*, at 80-1, 125; *IG Report II*, at 29-30.

[127] S. 1215, §2(b); H.R. 3361/S. 1599 §505(a). The text of the NSL statutes, now and in the form to which they would be returned, is appended.

[128] H.R. 3361/S. 1599 §505(b)("Notwithstanding subsection (a), the provisions of law referred to in subsection (a), as in effect on May 31, 2015, shall continue to apply on and after June 1, 2015, with respect to any particular foreign intelligence investigation or with respect to any particular offense or potential offense that began or occurred before (continued...)

The USA PATRIOT Act expanded existing authority under 18 U.S.C. 2709, the Right to Financial Privacy Act, and the Fair Credit Reporting Act.[129] It did not expand the reach of the National Security Act NSL statute. A return to the state of the law prior to enactment of the USA PATRIOT Act would have the effect of eliminating the amendments it made in the pre-existing NSL statutes.

In general terms for the three pre-existing NSL statutes that the USA PATRIOT Act amended, the Act:

- expanded issuing authority to include the heads of FBI field offices (special agents in charge (SACs));

- eliminated the requirement of specific and articulable facts demonstrating a nexus to a foreign power or its agents;

- required instead that the information was sought for or relevant to various national security investigations; and

- directed that no NSL-related investigation of a "U.S. person" (American citizen or foreign resident alien) be predicated exclusively on First Amendment protected activities.[130]

This meant that:

- NSLs were more readily available to FBI field agents at a lower level of supervisory control;

- NSLs could be used to obtain information pertaining to individuals two, three, or more steps removed from the foreign power or agent of a foreign power that is the focus of the investigation; and

- NSL-related investigations could not be predicated solely on the basis of activities protected by the First Amendment.

A return to the state of the law prior to the effective date of the USA PATRIOT Act would mean that NSLs would need to be approved by the FBI Director or a senior FBI headquarters official, and they would have to be based on specific and articulable facts giving reason to believe that the information sought pertains to a foreign power or agent of a foreign power.[131]

The language precluding NSL-related investigations grounded exclusively on the exercise of First Amendment rights would also disappear. It is at best unclear, however, that the First Amendment unaided does not embody a comparable prohibition.

Prior to the USA PATRIOT Act, the NSL statutes strictly prohibited recipients from disclosing the request to anyone, ever.[132] Yet, they afforded recipients no explicit means to challenge or seek

---

(...continued)

June 1, 2015"); similar language appears in S. 1215, §2(b)(2).

[129] P.L. 107-56, §505, 115 Stat. 365 (2001).

[130] 18 U.S.C. 2709((b), 12 U.S.C. 3414(a)(5)(A), 15 U.S.C. 1681u(a).

[131] 18 U.S.C. 2709((b)(2000 ed.), 12 U.S.C. 3414(a)(5)(A)(2000 ed.), 15 U.S.C. 1681u(a)(2000 ed.).

[132] 12 U.S.C. 3414(a)(5)(D)(2000 ed.); 15 U.S.C. 1681u(d)(2000 ed.); 18 U.S.C. 2709(c)(2000 ed.); 50 U.S.C. 436(b) (continued...)

limited release from the nondisclosure requirement,[133] even for such narrow purposes as consulting their attorneys for advice on their obligations to comply. On the other hand, they provided the FBI with no explicit remedy should recipients violate the nondisclosure requirement.

In the USA PATRIOT Improvement and Reauthorization Act, Congress addressed the issue in three ways. First, it amended the federal obstruction of justice statute to outlaw unjustified disclosures.[134] Second, it amended the NSL statutes to make it clear that a recipient remained free to seek the advice of counsel before complying.[135] These amendments, unlike the obstruction of justice amendment, would disappear should the NSL statutes return to their earlier versions. Congress's third response, however, would mitigate impact of the disappearance. Third, Congress created a permanent statutory section for review of NSLs, 18 U.S.C. 3511.

By and large, §3511 governs judicial review of NSL nondisclosure requirements. When implemented as required by the Second Circuit's decision in *John Doe, Inc. v. Mukasey*, 549 F.3d 861 (2d Cir. 2008), and at the election of the recipient, the government has the burden of persuading the court of the validity of the gag order under the same standards as found in the expired portions of the NSL statutes. S. 1215 and H.R. 3361/S. 1599's amendments to the judicial review provisions in §3511, designed to accommodate the concerns raised in *John Doe, Inc.*, would remain in effect after sunset.

The National Security Act NSL statute, left unamended by the USA PATRIOT Act, is arguably the least intrusive. It reaches only information pertaining to federal employees who have consented to their disclosure.[136]

When the Senate Judiciary Committee approved comparable provisions in the 112th Congress, it explained that:

> [S]unset was added not as an expression of desire for the authority to expire, but to guarantee that Congress [would] carefully review how NSLs are issued. After the standard for issuing an NSL was lowered in 2001, the use of NSLs spiked. Fewer than 10,000 NSLs were issued in 2001, but nearly 50,0000 were issued in 2006. Seeing the growth, Congress included Inspector General audits of NSLs in the 2005 USA PATIROT Act Reauthorization bill. The audits showed vast over-collection of information and abuse of the NSL authority.[137]

The Minority Views in the Senate Judiciary Committee report objected to a return of the NSL statutes to their earlier versions:

> S. 193 rescinds these valuable tools by, starting in 2013, requiring the government to follow the cumbersome pre-PATRIOT Act NSL standard. Prior to the PATRIOT Act, not only did

---

(...continued)

(2000 ed.).

[133] Depending upon one's perspective these provisions may be described as nondisclosure provisions, secrecy provisions, or gag order provisions. The descriptions are used interchangeably without any intended connotations in this report.

[134] 18 U.S.C. 1510(e).

[135] 12 U.S.C. 3414(a)(5)(D); 15 U.S.C. 1681u(d); 18 U.S.C. 2709(c); 50 U.S.C. 3162(b).

[136] 50 U.S.C. 3162(a)(3)(A).

[137] S.Rept. 112-13, at 15 (2001).

the requested records have to be relevant to an investigation, but the FBI also had to have specific and articulable facts giving reason to believe that the information requested pertained to a foreign power or an agent of a foreign power, such as a terrorist or spy. This pre-PATRIOT Act requirement kept the FBI from using NSLs to develop evidence at the early stages of an investigation, which is precisely when they are the most useful, and often prevented investigators from acquiring records that were relevant to an ongoing international terrorism or espionage investigation.

It makes little sense to roll back the sensible NSL reforms that were made as part of the USA PATRIOT Act. Criminal investigators have long been able to use administrative or grand jury subpoenas to obtain records, so long as they are relevant to their investigation.[138]

Text of NSL Statutes on October 25, 2001, and Now (emphasis added)

12 U.S.C. 3414(a)(5) (on October 25, 2001)

* * *

(a) ....

(5)(A) Financial institutions, and officers, employees, and agents thereof, shall comply with a request for a customer's or entity's financial records made pursuant to this subsection by the Federal Bureau of Investigation when the Director of the Federal Bureau of Investigation (or the Director's designee) certifies in writing to the financial institution that such records are sought for foreign counter intelligence purposes *and that there are specific and articulable facts giving reason to believe that the customer or entity whose records are sought is a foreign power or the agents of a foreign power as defined in section 1801 of title 50.*

(B) The Federal Bureau of Investigation may disseminate information obtained pursuant to this paragraph only as provided in guidelines approved by the Attorney General for foreign intelligence collection and foreign counterintelligence investigations conducted by the Federal Bureau of Investigation, and, with respect to dissemination to an agency of the United States, only if such information is clearly relevant to the authorized responsibilities of such agency.

(C) On a semiannual basis the Attorney General shall fully inform the Permanent Select Committee on Intelligence of the House of Representatives and the Select Committee on Intelligence of the Senate concerning all requests made pursuant to this paragraph.

(D) No financial institution, or officer, employee, or agent of such institution, shall disclose to any person that the Federal Bureau of Investigation has sought or obtained access to a customer's or entity's financial records under this paragraph.

---

[138] *Id.* at 41-2 (Minority Views). Although they are both available in terrorism investigations, NSLs and grand jury subpoenas are not completely analogous, for example recipients of grand jury subpoenas are not ordinarily bound by the grand jury secrecy rules, see e.g., F.R.Crim.P. 6(e)(2)(A)("No obligation of secrecy may be imposed on any person except in accordance with Rule 6(e)(2)(B)"); *United States v. Sells Engineering, Inc.,* 463 U.S. 418, 425 (1983)("Witnesses are not under the prohibition unless they also happen to fit into one of the enumerated classes [i.e., grand juror, interpreter, court reporter, attorney for the government, and the like]"); *Butterworth v. Smith,* 494 U.S. 624 (1990)(holding unconstitutional, as a violation of the First Amendment, a Florida statute that prohibited a witness from ever disclosing his or her grand jury testimony).

12 U.S.C. 3414(a)(5) (now)

* * *

(a) ...

(5)(A) Financial institutions, and officers, employees, and agents thereof, shall comply with a request for a customer's or entity's financial records made pursuant to this subsection by the Federal Bureau of Investigation when the Director of the Federal Bureau of Investigation (or the Director's designee *in a position not lower than Deputy Assistant Director at Bureau headquarters or a Special Agent in Charge in a Bureau field office designated by the Director*) certifies in writing to the financial institution that such records are sought for foreign counter intelligence purposes *to protect against international terrorism or clandestine intelligence activities, provided that such an investigation of a United States person is not conducted solely upon the basis of activities protected by the first amendment to the Constitution of the United States.*

(B) The Federal Bureau of Investigation may disseminate information obtained pursuant to this paragraph only as provided in guidelines approved by the Attorney General for foreign intelligence collection and foreign counterintelligence investigations conducted by the Federal Bureau of Investigation, and, with respect to dissemination to an agency of the United States, only if such information is clearly relevant to the authorized responsibilities of such agency.

(C) On the dates provided in section 415b of Title 50, the Attorney General shall fully inform the congressional intelligence committees (as defined in section 401a of Title 50) concerning all requests made pursuant to this paragraph.

(D) Prohibition of certain disclosure.—

(i) *If the Director of the Federal Bureau of Investigation, or his designee in a position not lower than Deputy Assistant Director at Bureau headquarters or a Special Agent in Charge in a Bureau field office designated by the Director, certifies that otherwise there may result a danger to the national security of the United States, interference with a criminal, counterterrorism, or counterintelligence investigation, interference with diplomatic relations, or danger to the life or physical safety of any person*, no financial institution, or officer, employee, or agent of such institution, shall disclose to any person *(other than those to whom such disclosure is necessary to comply with the request or an attorney to obtain legal advice or legal assistance with respect to the request)* that the Federal Bureau of Investigation has sought or obtained access to a customer's or entity's financial records under subparagraph (A).

(ii) *The request shall notify the person or entity to whom the request is directed of the nondisclosure requirement under clause (i).*

(iii) *Any recipient disclosing to those persons necessary to comply with the request or to an attorney to obtain legal advice or legal assistance with respect to the request shall inform such persons of any applicable nondisclosure requirement. Any person who receives a disclosure under this subsection shall be subject to the same prohibitions on disclosure under clause (i).*

(iv) *At the request of the Director of the Federal Bureau of Investigation or the designee of the Director, any person making or intending to make a disclosure under this section shall identify to the Director or such designee the person to whom such disclosure will be made or to whom such disclosure was made prior to the request, except that nothing in this section shall require a person to inform the Director or such designee of the identity of an attorney to whom disclosure was made or will be made to obtain legal advice or legal assistance with respect to the request for financial records under subparagraph (A).*

15 U.S.C. 1681u(a), (b)(on October 25, 2001)

(a) Identity of financial institutions

Notwithstanding section 1681b of this title or any other provision of this subchapter, a consumer reporting agency shall furnish to the Federal Bureau of Investigation the names and addresses of all financial institutions (as that term is defined in section 3401 of Title 12) at which a consumer maintains or has maintained an account, to the extent that information is in the files of the agency, when presented with a written request for that information, signed by the Director of the Federal Bureau of Investigation, or the Director's designee, which certifies compliance with this section. The Director or the Director's designee may make such a certification only if the Director or the Director's designee has determined in writing that—

(1) such information is necessary for the conduct of an authorized foreign counterintelligence investigation; and

(2) there are specific and articulable facts giving reason to believe that the consumer—

(A) is a foreign power (as defined in section 1801 of title 50) or a person who is not a United States person (as defined in such section 1801 of title 50) and is an official of a foreign power; or

(B) is an agent of a foreign power and is engaging or has engaged in an act of international terrorism (as that term is defined in section 1801(c) of title 50) or clandestine intelligence activities that involve or may involve a violation of criminal statutes of the United States.

(b) Identifying information

Notwithstanding the provisions of section 1681b of this title or any other provision of this subchapter, a consumer reporting agency shall furnish identifying information respecting a consumer, limited to name, address, former addresses, places of employment, or former places of employment, to the Federal Bureau of Investigation when presented with a written request, signed by the Director or the Director's designee, which certifies compliance with this subsection. The Director or the Director's designee may make such a certification only if the Director or the Director's designee has determined in writing that—

(1) such information is necessary to the conduct of an authorized counterintelligence investigation; and

(2) there is information giving reason to believe that the consumer has been, or is about to be, in contact with a foreign power or an agent of a foreign power (as defined in section 1801 of title 50).

* * *

15 U.S.C. 1681u(a), (b)(now)

(a) Identity of financial institutions

Notwithstanding section 1681b of this title or any other provision of this subchapter, a consumer reporting agency shall furnish to the Federal Bureau of Investigation the names and addresses of all financial institutions (as that term is defined in section 3401 of Title 12) at which a consumer maintains or has maintained an account, to the extent that information is in the files of the agency, when presented with a written request for that information, signed by the Director of the Federal Bureau of Investigation, or the Director's designee *in a position not lower than Deputy Assistant Director at Bureau headquarters or a Special Agent in Charge of a Bureau field office designated by the Director*, which certifies compliance with this section. The Director or the Director's designee may make such a certification only if the Director or the Director's designee has determined in writing, that *such information is sought for the conduct of an authorized investigation to protect against international terrorism or clandestine intelligence activities, provided that such an investigation of a United States person is not conducted solely upon the basis of activities protected by the first amendment to the Constitution of the United States.*

(b) Identifying information

 Notwithstanding the provisions of section 1681b of this title or any other provision of this subchapter, a consumer reporting agency shall furnish identifying information respecting a consumer, limited to name, address, former addresses, places of employment, or former places of employment, to the Federal Bureau of Investigation when presented with a written request, signed by the Director or the Director's designee *in a position not lower than Deputy Assistant Director at Bureau headquarters or a Special Agent in Charge of a Bureau field office designated by the Director*, which certifies compliance with this subsection. The Director or the Director's designee may make such a certification only if the Director or the Director's designee has determined in writing that *such information is sought for the conduct of an authorized investigation to protect against international terrorism or clandestine intelligence activities, provided that such an investigation of a United States person is not conducted solely upon the basis of activities protected by the first amendment to the Constitution of the United States.*

* * *

18 U.S.C. 2709 (as of October 25, 2001)

(a) Duty to provide.—A wire or electronic communication service provider shall comply with a request for subscriber information and toll billing records information, or electronic communication transactional records in its custody or possession made by the Director of the Federal Bureau of Investigation under subsection (b) of this section.

(b) Required certification.—The Director of the Federal Bureau of Investigation, or his designee in a position not lower than Deputy Assistant Director, may—

 (1) request the name, address, length of service, and local and long distance toll billing records of a person or entity if the Director (or his designee in a position not lower than Deputy Assistant Director) certifies in writing to the wire or electronic communication service provider to which the request is made that—

   (A) the name, address, length of service, and toll billing records sought are relevant to an authorized foreign counterintelligence investigation; and

   (B) there are specific and articulable facts giving reason to believe that the person or entity to whom the information sought pertains is a foreign power or an agent of a foreign power as defined in section 101 of the Foreign intelligence Surveillance Act of 1978 (50 U.S.C. 1801); and

 (2) request the name, address, and length of service of a person or entity if the Director (or his designee in a position not lower than Deputy Assistant Director) certifies in writing to the wire or electronic communication service provider to which the request is made that—

   (A) the information sought is relevant to an authorized foreign counterintelligence investigation; and

   (B) there are specific and articulable facts giving reason to believe that communication facilities registered in the name of the person or entity have been used, through the services of such provider, in communications with—

     (i) an individual who is engaging or has engaged in international terrorism as defined in section 101(c) of the Foreign Intelligence Surveillance Act or clandestine intelligence

activities that involve or may involve a violation of the criminal statutes of the United States; or

(ii) a foreign power or agent of a foreign power under circumstances giving reason to believe that the communication concerned international terrorism as defined in section 101(c) of the Foreign Intelligence Surveillance Act or clandestine intelligence activities that involve or may involve a violation of the criminal statutes of the United States.

(c) Prohibition of certain disclosure.—No wire or electronic communication service provider, or officer, employee, or agent thereof, shall disclose to any person that the Federal Bureau of Investigation has sought or obtained access to information or records under this section.

(d) Dissemination by bureau.—The Federal Bureau of Investigation may disseminate information and records obtained under this section only as provided in guidelines approved by the Attorney General for foreign intelligence collection and foreign counterintelligence investigations conducted by the Federal Bureau of Investigation, and, with respect to dissemination to an agency of the United States, only if such information is clearly relevant to the authorized responsibilities of such agency.

(e) Requirement that certain congressional bodies be informed.—On a semiannual basis the Director of the Federal Bureau of Investigation shall fully inform the Permanent Select Committee on Intelligence of the House of Representatives and the Select Committee on Intelligence of the Senate, and the Committee on the Judiciary of the House of Representatives and the Committee on the Judiciary of the Senate, concerning all requests made under subsection (b) of this section.

18 U.S.C. 2709 (now)

(a) Duty to provide.—A wire or electronic communication service provider shall comply with a request for subscriber information and toll billing records information, or electronic communication transactional records in its custody or possession made by the Director of the Federal Bureau of Investigation under subsection (b) of this section.

(b) Required certification.—The Director of the Federal Bureau of Investigation, or his designee in a position not lower than Deputy Assistant Director *at Bureau headquarters or a Special Agent in Charge in a Bureau field office designated by the Director*, may—

(1) request the name, address, length of service, and local and long distance toll billing records of a person or entity if the Director (or his designee) certifies in writing to the wire or electronic communication service provider to which the request is made that the name, address, length of service, and toll billing records *sought are relevant to an authorized investigation to protect against international terrorism or clandestine intelligence activities, provided that such an investigation of a United States person is not conducted solely on the basis of activities protected by the first amendment to the Constitution of the United States*; and

(2) request the name, address, and length of service of a person or entity if the Director (or his designee) certifies in writing to the wire or electronic communication service provider to which the request is made that the information *sought is relevant to an authorized investigation to protect against international terrorism or clandestine intelligence activities, provided that such an investigation of a United States person is not conducted solely upon the basis of activities protected by the first amendment to the Constitution of the United States.*

(c) Prohibition of certain disclosure.—

(1) If the Director of the Federal Bureau of Investigation, or his designee in a position not lower than Deputy Assistant Director at Bureau headquarters or a Special Agent in Charge in a Bureau field office designated by the Director, certifies that otherwise there may result a danger to the national security of the United States, interference with a criminal, counterterrorism, or counterintelligence investigation, interference with diplomatic relations, or danger to the life or physical safety of any person, no wire or electronic communications service provider, or officer, employee, or agent thereof, shall disclose to any person (other than those to whom such disclosure is necessary to comply with the request or an attorney to obtain legal advice or legal assistance with respect to the request) that the Federal Bureau of Investigation has sought or obtained access to information or records under this section.

(2) The request shall notify the person or entity to whom the request is directed of the nondisclosure requirement under paragraph (1).

(3) Any recipient disclosing to those persons necessary to comply with the request or to an attorney to obtain legal advice or legal assistance with respect to the request shall inform such person of any applicable nondisclosure requirement. Any person who receives a disclosure under this subsection shall be subject to the same prohibitions on disclosure under paragraph (1).

(4) At the request of the Director of the Federal Bureau of Investigation or the designee of the Director, any person making or intending to make a disclosure under this section shall identify to the Director or such designee the person to whom such disclosure will be made or to whom such disclosure was made prior to the request, except that nothing in this section shall require a person to inform the Director or such designee of the identity of an attorney to whom disclosure was made or will be made to obtain legal advice or legal assistance with respect to the request under subsection (a).

(d) Dissemination by bureau.—The Federal Bureau of Investigation may disseminate information and records obtained under this section only as provided in guidelines approved by the Attorney General for foreign intelligence collection and foreign counterintelligence investigations conducted by the Federal Bureau of Investigation, and, with respect to dissemination to an agency of the United States, only if such information is clearly relevant to the authorized responsibilities of such agency.

(e) Requirement that certain congressional bodies be informed.—On a semiannual basis the Director of the Federal Bureau of Investigation shall fully inform the Permanent Select Committee on Intelligence of the House of Representatives and the Select Committee on Intelligence of the Senate, and the Committee on the Judiciary of the House of Representatives and the Committee on the Judiciary of the Senate, concerning all requests made under subsection (b) of this section.

(f) Libraries.—A library (as that term is defined in section 213(1) of the Library Services and Technology Act (20 U.S.C. 9122(1)), the services of which include access to the Internet, books, journals, magazines, newspapers, or other similar forms of communication in print or digitally by patrons for their use, review, examination, or circulation, is not a wire or electronic communication service provider for purposes of this section, unless the library is providing the services defined in section 2510(15) ("electronic communication service") of this title.

15 U.S.C. 1681v (as of October 25, 2001)

NONE. This section was created by the USA PATRIOT Act, effective October 26, 2001.

15 U.S.C. 1681v (now)

(a) Disclosure

Notwithstanding section 1681b of this title or any other provision of this subchapter, a consumer reporting agency shall furnish a consumer report of a consumer and all other information in a consumer's file to a government agency authorized to conduct investigations of, or intelligence or counterintelligence activities or analysis related to, international terrorism when presented with a written certification by such government agency that such information is necessary for the agency's conduct or such investigation, activity or analysis.

(b) Form of certification

The certification described in subsection (a) of this section shall be signed by a supervisory official designated by the head of a Federal agency or an officer of a Federal agency whose appointment to office is required to be made by the President, by and with the advice and consent of the Senate.

(c) Confidentiality

(1) If the head of a government agency authorized to conduct investigations of intelligence or counterintelligence activities or analysis related to international terrorism, or his designee, certifies that otherwise there may result a danger to the national security of the United States, interference with a criminal, counterterrorism, or counterintelligence investigation, interference with diplomatic relations, or danger to the life or physical safety of any person, no consumer reporting agency or officer, employee, or agent of such consumer reporting agency, shall disclose to any person (other than those to whom such disclosure is necessary to comply with the request or an attorney to obtain legal advice or legal assistance with respect to the request), or specify in any consumer report, that a government agency has sought or obtained access to information under subsection (a) of this section.

(2) The request shall notify the person or entity to whom the request is directed of the nondisclosure requirement under paragraph (1).

(3) Any recipient disclosing to those persons necessary to comply with the request or to any attorney to obtain legal advice or legal assistance with respect to the request shall inform such persons of any applicable nondisclosure requirement. Any person who receives a disclosure under this subsection shall be subject to the same prohibitions on disclosure under paragraph (1).

(4) At the request of the authorized government agency, any person making or intending to make a disclosure under this section shall identify to the requesting official of the authorized government agency the person to whom such disclosure will be made or to whom such disclosure was made prior to the request, except that nothing in this section shall require a person to inform the requesting official of the identity of an attorney to whom disclosure was made or will be made to obtain legal advice or legal assistance with respect to the request for information under subsection (a) of this section.

(d) Rule of construction

Nothing in section 1681u of this title shall be construed to limit the authority of the Director of the Federal Bureau of Investigation under this section.

(e) Safe harbor

Notwithstanding any other provision of this subchapter, any consumer reporting agency or agent or employee thereof making disclosure of consumer reports or other information pursuant to this section in good-faith reliance upon a certification of a government agency pursuant to the provisions of this section shall not be liable to any person for such disclosure under this subchapter, the constitution of any State, or any law or regulation of any State or any political subdivision of any State.

(f) Reports to Congress

(1) On a semi-annual basis, the Attorney General shall fully inform the Committee on the Judiciary, the Committee on Financial Services, and the Permanent Select Committee on Intelligence of the House of Representatives and the Committee on the Judiciary, the Committee on Banking, Housing, and Urban Affairs, and the Select Committee on Intelligence of the Senate concerning all requests made pursuant to subsection (a) of this section.

(2) In the case of the semiannual reports required to be submitted under paragraph (1) to the Permanent Select Committee on Intelligence of the House of Representatives and the Select Committee on Intelligence of the Senate, the submittal dates for such reports shall be as provided in section 415b of Title 50.

Sec. 802 of the National Security Act (50 U.S.C. 436 (as of October 25, 2001)

(a) Generally

(1) Any authorized investigative agency may request from any financial agency, financial institution, or holding company, or from any consumer reporting agency, such financial records, other financial information, and consumer reports as may be necessary in order to conduct any authorized law enforcement investigation, counterintelligence inquiry, or security determination. Any authorized investigative agency may also request records maintained by any commercial entity within the United States pertaining to travel by an employee in the executive branch of Government outside the United States.

(2) Requests may be made under this section where—

(A) the records sought pertain to a person who is or was an employee in the executive branch of Government required by the President in an Executive order or regulation, as a condition of access to classified information, to provide consent, during a background investigation and for such time as access to the information is maintained, and for a period of not more than three years thereafter, permitting access to financial records, other financial information, consumer reports, and travel records; and

(B)(i) there are reasonable grounds to believe, based on credible information, that the person is, or may be, disclosing classified information in an unauthorized manner to a foreign power or agent of a foreign power;

(ii) information the employing agency deems credible indicates the person has incurred excessive indebtedness or has acquired a level of affluence which cannot be explained by other information known to the agency; or

(iii) circumstances indicate the person had the capability and opportunity to disclose classified information which is known to have been lost or compromised to a foreign power or an agent of a foreign power.

(3) Each such request—

(A) shall be accompanied by a written certification signed by the department or agency head or deputy department or agency head concerned, or by a senior official designated for this purpose by the department or agency head concerned (whose rank shall be no lower than Assistant Secretary or Assistant Director), and shall certify that—

(i) the person concerned is or was an employee within the meaning of paragraph (2)(A);

(ii) the request is being made pursuant to an authorized inquiry or investigation and is authorized under this section; and

(iii) the records or information to be reviewed are records or information which the employee has previously agreed to make available to the authorized investigative agency for review;

(B) shall contain a copy of the agreement referred to in subparagraph (A)(iii);

(C) shall identify specifically or by category the records or information to be reviewed; and

(D) shall inform the recipient of the request of the prohibition described in subsection (b) of this section.

(b) *Disclosure of requests*

Notwithstanding any other provision of law, no governmental or private entity, or officer, employee, or agent of such entity, may disclose to any person that such entity has received or satisfied a request made by an authorized investigative agency under this section.

* * *

Sec. 802 of the National Security Act (50 U.S.C. 3162 (now))

(a) Generally

(1) Any authorized investigative agency may request from any financial agency, financial institution, or holding company, or from any consumer reporting agency, such financial records, other financial information, and consumer reports as may be necessary in order to conduct any authorized law enforcement investigation, counterintelligence inquiry, or security determination. Any authorized investigative agency may also request records maintained by any commercial entity within the United States pertaining to travel by an employee in the executive branch of Government outside the United States.

(2) Requests may be made under this section where—

(A) the records sought pertain to a person who is or was an employee in the executive branch of Government required by the President in an Executive order or regulation, as a condition of access to classified information, to provide consent, during a background investigation and for such time as access to the information is maintained, and for a period of not more than three years thereafter, permitting access to financial records, other financial information, consumer reports, and travel records; and

(B)(i) there are reasonable grounds to believe, based on credible information, that the person is, or may be, disclosing classified information in an unauthorized manner to a foreign power or agent of a foreign power;

(ii) information the employing agency deems credible indicates the person has incurred excessive indebtedness or has acquired a level of affluence which cannot be explained by other information known to the agency; or

(iii) circumstances indicate the person had the capability and opportunity to disclose classified information which is known to have been lost or compromised to a foreign power or an agent of a foreign power.

(3) Each such request—

(A) shall be accompanied by a written certification signed by the department or agency head or deputy department or agency head concerned, or by a senior official designated for this purpose by the department or agency head concerned (whose rank shall be no lower than Assistant Secretary or Assistant Director), and shall certify that—

(i) the person concerned is or was an employee within the meaning of paragraph (2)(A);

(ii) the request is being made pursuant to an authorized inquiry or investigation and is authorized under this section; and

(iii) the records or information to be reviewed are records or information which the employee has previously agreed to make available to the authorized investigative agency for review;

(B) shall contain a copy of the agreement referred to in subparagraph (A)(iii);

(C) shall identify specifically or by category the records or information to be reviewed; and

(D) shall inform the recipient of the request of the prohibition described in subsection (b) of this section.

(b) Prohibition of certain disclosure

(1) If an authorized investigative agency described in subsection (a) of this section certifies that otherwise there may result a danger to the national security of the United States, interference with a criminal, counterterrorism, or counterintelligence investigation, interference with diplomatic relations, or danger to the life or physical safety of any person, no governmental or private entity, or officer, employee, or agent of such entity, may disclose to any person (other than those to whom such disclosure is necessary to comply with the request or an attorney to obtain legal advice or legal assistance with respect to the request) that such entity has received or satisfied a request made by an authorized investigative agency under this section.

(2) The request shall notify the person or entity to whom the request is directed of the nondisclosure requirement under paragraph (1).

(3) Any recipient disclosing to those persons necessary to comply with the request or to an attorney to obtain legal advice or legal assistance with respect to the request shall inform such persons of any applicable nondisclosure requirement. Any person who receives a disclosure under this subsection shall be subject to the same prohibitions on disclosure under paragraph (1).

(4) At the request of the authorized investigative agency, any person making or intending to make a disclosure under this section shall identify to the requesting official of the authorized investigative agency the person to whom such disclosure will be made or to whom such disclosure was made prior to the request, except that nothing in this section shall require a person to inform the requesting official of the identity of an attorney to whom disclosure was made or will be made to obtain legal advice or legal assistance with respect to the request under subsection (a) of this section.

* * *

P.L. 109-177, Sec. 118 (text)

Reports on National Security Letters.

(a) Existing Reports—Any report made to a committee of Congress regarding national security letters under section 2709(c)(1) of title 18, United States Code, sections 626(d) or 627(c) of the Fair Credit Reporting Act (15 U.S.C. 1681u(d) or 1681v(c)), section 1114(a)(3) or 1114(a)(5)(D) of the Right to Financial Privacy Act (12 U.S.C. 3414(a)(3) or 3414(a)(5)(D)), or section 802(b) of the National Security Act of 1947 (50 U.S.C. [3126](b)) shall also be made to the Committees on the Judiciary of the House of Representatives and the Senate.

* * *

(c) Report on Requests for National Security Letters-

(1) IN GENERAL- In April of each year, the Attorney General shall submit to Congress an aggregate report setting forth with respect to the preceding year the total number of requests made by the Department of Justice for information concerning different United States persons under—

    (A) section 2709 of title 18, United States Code (to access certain communication service provider records), excluding the number of requests for subscriber information;

    (B) section 1114 of the Right to Financial Privacy Act (12 U.S.C. 3414) (to obtain financial institution customer records);

    (C) section 802 of the National Security Act of 1947 (50 U.S.C. [3126]) (to obtain financial information, records, and consumer reports);

    (D) section 626 of the Fair Credit Reporting Act (15 U.S.C. 1681u) (to obtain certain financial information and consumer reports); and

    (E) section 627 of the Fair Credit Reporting Act (15 U.S.C. 1681v) (to obtain credit agency consumer records for counterterrorism investigations).

(2) UNCLASSIFIED FORM- The report under this section shall be submitted in unclassified form.

(d) National Security Letter Defined- In this section, the term 'national security letter' means a request for information under one of the following provisions of law:

(1) Section 2709(a) of title 18, United States Code (to access certain communication service provider records).

(2) Section 1114(a)(5)(A) of the Right to Financial Privacy Act (12 U.S.C. 3414(a)(5)(A)) (to obtain financial institution customer records).

(3) Section 802 of the National Security Act of 1947 (50 U.S.C.[3162]) (to obtain financial information, records, and consumer reports).

(4) Section 626 of the Fair Credit Reporting Act (15 U.S.C. 1681u) (to obtain certain financial information and consumer reports).

(5) Section 627 of the Fair Credit Reporting Act (15 U.S.C. 1681v) (to obtain credit agency consumer records for counterterrorism investigations).

P.L. 109-177, Sec. 119 (text)

Audit of Use of National Security Letters.

(a) Audit—The Inspector General of the Department of Justice shall perform an audit of the effectiveness and use, including any improper or illegal use, of national security letters issued by the Department of Justice.

(b) Requirements- The audit required under subsection (a) shall include—

(1) an examination of the use of national security letters by the Department of Justice during calendar years 2003 through 2006;

(2) a description of any noteworthy facts or circumstances relating to such use, including any improper or illegal use of such authority; and

(3) an examination of the effectiveness of national security letters as an investigative tool, including—

    (A) the importance of the information acquired by the Department of Justice to the intelligence activities of the Department of Justice or to any other department or agency of the Federal Government;

    (B) the manner in which such information is collected, retained, analyzed, and disseminated by the Department of Justice, including any direct access to such information (such as access to 'raw data') provided to any other department, agency, or instrumentality of Federal, State, local, or tribal governments or any private sector entity;

(C) whether, and how often, the Department of Justice utilized such information to produce an analytical intelligence product for distribution within the Department of Justice, to the intelligence community (as such term is defined in section 3(4) of the National Security Act of 1947 (50 U.S.C. 401a(4))), or to other Federal, State, local, or tribal government departments, agencies, or instrumentalities;

(D) whether, and how often, the Department of Justice provided such information to law enforcement authorities for use in criminal proceedings;

(E) with respect to national security letters issued following the date of the enactment of this Act, an examination of the number of occasions in which the Department of Justice, or an officer or employee of the Department of Justice, issued a national security letter without the certification necessary to require the recipient of such letter to comply with the nondisclosure and confidentiality requirements potentially applicable under law; and

(F) the types of electronic communications and transactional information obtained through requests for information under section 2709 of title 18, United States Code, including the types of dialing, routing, addressing, or signaling information obtained, and the procedures the Department of Justice uses if content information is obtained through the use of such authority.

(c) Submission Dates-

(1) PRIOR YEARS- Not later than one year after the date of the enactment of this Act, or upon completion of the audit under this section for calendar years 2003 and 2004, whichever is earlier, the Inspector General of the Department of Justice shall submit to the Committee on the Judiciary and the Permanent Select Committee on Intelligence of the House of Representatives and the Committee on the Judiciary and the Select Committee on Intelligence of the Senate a report containing the results of the audit conducted under this subsection for calendar years 2003 and 2004.

(2) CALENDAR YEARS 2005 AND 2006- Not later than December 31, 2007, or upon completion of the audit under this subsection for calendar years 2005 and 2006, whichever is earlier, the Inspector General of the Department of Justice shall submit to the Committee on the Judiciary and the Permanent Select Committee on Intelligence of the House of Representatives and the Committee on the Judiciary and the Select Committee on Intelligence of the Senate a report containing the results of the audit conducted under this subsection for calendar years 2005 and 2006.

(d) Prior Notice to Attorney General and Director of National Intelligence; Comments-

(1) NOTICE- Not less than 30 days before the submission of a report under subsections (c)(1) or (c)(2), the Inspector General of the Department of Justice shall provide such report to the Attorney General and the Director of National Intelligence.

(2) COMMENTS- The Attorney General or the Director of National Intelligence may provide comments to be included in the reports submitted under subsections (c)(1) or (c)(2) as the Attorney General or the Director of National Intelligence may consider necessary.

(e) Unclassified Form- The reports submitted under subsections (c)(1) or (c)(2) and any comments included under subsection (d)(2) shall be in unclassified form, but may include a classified annex.

(f) Minimization Procedures Feasibility- Not later than February 1, 2007, or upon completion of review of the report submitted under subsection (c)(1), whichever is earlier, the Attorney General and the Director of National Intelligence shall jointly submit to the Committee on the Judiciary and the Permanent Select Committee on Intelligence of the House of Representatives and the Committee on the Judiciary and the Select Committee on Intelligence of the Senate a report on the feasibility of applying minimization procedures in the context of national security letters to ensure the protection of the constitutional rights of United States persons.

(g) National Security Letter Defined- In this section, the term 'national security letter' means a request for information under one of the following provisions of law:
 (1) Section 2709(a) of title 18, United States Code (to access certain communication service provider records).
 (2) Section 1114(a)(5)(A) of the Right to Financial Privacy Act (12 U.S.C. 3414(a)(5)(A)) (to obtain financial institution customer records).
 (3) Section 802 of the National Security Act of 1947 (50 U.S.C. 436) (to obtain financial information, records, and consumer reports).
 (4) Section 626 of the Fair Credit Reporting Act (15 U.S.C. 1681u) (to obtain certain financial information and consumer reports).

 (5) Section 627 of the Fair Credit Reporting Act (15 U.S.C. 1681v) (to obtain credit agency consumer records for counterterrorism investigations).

Author Contact Information

Charles Doyle
Senior Specialist in American Public Law
cdoyle@crs.loc.gov, 7-6968